IT'S ALL IN YOUR HEAD

AN INTERACTIVE THOUGHT CHALLENGE
TO ACHIEVING YOUR BEST YOU

CLIFF WILT

Cliff Wilt
Chicago, IL 60506
cliff@cliffwilt.com
www.cliffwilt.com

Limits of Liability and Disclaimer of Warranty

The author and publisher shall not be liable for your misuse of this material. This book is strictly for informational and educational purposes.

Warning – Disclaimer

The purpose of this book is to educate and entertain. The author and/or publisher do not guarantee that anyone following these techniques, suggestions, tips, ideas, or strategies will become successful. The author and/or publisher shall have neither liability nor responsibility to anyone with respect to any loss or damage caused, or alleged to be caused, directly or indirectly by the information contained in this book. All quotes are attributed to the author to the best of public knowledge. Any images are either in public domain or from royalty free sites. If you find a discrepancy, please feel free to contact the author at cliff@cliffwilt.com. It is never the author's intention to misuse any kind of intellectual property

Free Bonus Resources

This book is full of some of the best tips and challenges to get you on the road to success through inspired transformational thinking.

I want you to succeed, and because of that, we have put together some free resources to help get you to become the personal success you desire to be. To get instant access to the free downloads, articles, and info, please visit:

www.cliffwilt.com

Acknowledgment/Dedication

Thank You to my wife Ana who inspires me everyday to keep growing, caring, and sharing.

I woud like to thank and acknowledge Donna Kozik, multiple award winning author, who's input and content suggestions helped bring this all together.

I dedicate this book to all who are willing to accept the challenge to challenge your own thinking and find strength and peace in the face of all circumstances within yourself. It starts with the mind!

About the Author

Cliff Wilt is a Certified Professional Coach for life and business.

He has traveled and worked giving talks and seminars in the United States and several countries worldwide. As a speaker and seminar leader, he addresses multiple areas for personal and relationship growth in life and business.

He has studied, researched, and spoken for years in the fields of personal development, business, philosophy and psychology. He speaks to public and corporate audiences on the subjects of Personal and Professional Development. His exciting talks and seminars on Leadership, Self-Esteem, Goals, Strategy, and Personal Success Psychology bring about immediate changes and long-lasting results.

Introduction

Congratulations for investing in yourself with the purchase of this book. I believe you will find it enjoyable and inspirational in helping you to know yourself in a deeper way and transform yourself in a profound way just as I have in using these very same challenges. I wrote this book because just as I as a resource want to everyday read something that would cause me to think and challenge myself to continually become a better more positive influencing version of the ultimate me, believe there are millions more that are up for the challenge.

It seems we are sometimes of the mindset that we are just fine the way we are and not in need of any change. Yet we find ourselves drained of our energy in many of the circumstances we face and believe it has nothing to do with us, but with everything else in our life. With that kind of thinking we have already lost sight of the fact that the relationship world is constantly in transformation, which means if we are not changing forward for positive impact, we are regressing into a plateaued existence that will be a miserable state to be in. This is as true for self as it is for the world around us.

Your greatest strength and weapon is your mind and how you think. It is where you initiate the resources available for you to actually engage in this gift we call 'LIFE'. Many times we fall prey to the traps that ensnare us in our thinking, because we are not consistently challenging these mind resources and thought processes to be the best updated, and cutting edge weaponry possible. We accomplish this through honest self examination, purposed education, and transformational thinking.

Thinking transformationally is what is needed to find strength and harmonious outcome in every situation. Your mind is your most valuable asset. One of the most precious skills you can have is to think well and objectively rise above self inflicted limitations to master successfully the best you possible.

I have personally used challenging thoughts consistently throughout my life. I put them in places where I will see them to inspire myself to be a better me today than I was the day before. It has been proven that our circumstances can change based on what words we read, hear, and speak. No matter where you are personally in life, you and your life situations can be positively transformed by the renewing of your mind.

I know what it is like to experience life altering failures and successes. I have accomplished both in my life. In the midst of failures and successes there are thoughts that come to mind that you have to challenge within yourself to rise above your circumstances in a way that will not only help you, but can in the future help others as well.

I have compiled some personal thoughts and quotes in this book that not only have helped me and others rise above personal challenges and become successful, but as a challenge for you to become more than you thought you could be as a positive force for yourself and to benefit those around you. This is not for the faint of heart for it will compel you to honestly assess yourself and then challenge yourself personally to develop a mindset and actions that will effectively impact you and the world around you.

You must be willing to think through each challenge and persevere relentlessly until you have reached purposed and beneficial resolutions.

Your only limits will be the ones you place on yourself. Here is a fact that will interest you. Studies have been done with proven results that the act of thinking, journaling, and implementation, forces you to use your mind at a higher level. So realistically, you actually become smarter.

Intrinsically these thoughts and challenges are for your benefit. It just so happens though that the ultimate unavoidable by-product of your transforming adventure will positively impact the world around you also.

In order to be successful at this the following elements must be employed at all times: You MUST ...

- *Desire-* Desire to be more than you are right now. Only a strong unbending desire will compel you to continually take the necessary steps.

  You MUST also make a ...

- *Decision-* Decide that there are no other options. You will make every effort, conquer any obstacle, and do whatever it takes to succeed at becoming a better you.

  You MUST Also commit to ...

- ***Discipline-*** Discipline yourself to plan, prepare, and execute the exercises over and over again, until you achieve success.

  You MUST Finally …

- ***Determine-*** Determine to persist and persevere. That you will not accept anything less than the absolute best YOU possible. Our fears and doubts are our worst enemies, however, You are infinitely more capable than you think. There are no limits except for the limits you place on yourself. So, grab on to your determination and let's do this together!

ARE YOU READY?

GREAT!

Let the Adventure begin!

Getting the most benefit from this book

INDIVIDUAL ~

Read one (or more – your preference) thought each day.

After reading the thought, start by writing down something/anything that you are grateful for. Starting each day with gratitude will already open your mind to infinite possibiliteis.

Based on the printed thought, think of what you can do to challenge yourself in your actions and your mindset to improve inregards to that particular subject. Some of the subjects may appear to be the same but they are not. The wording is done in such a way as to get your mind to think expandedly which will help you to advance in life and relationships, beyond what you even thought was possible.

I would also recommend that after you finish each challenge you chose, that you take a few moments to meditate on what you wrote as a challenge to yourself to improve on, and for what you may have learned through the process. You could play some soft intstrumental music while you meditate to keep yourself focused. Take some deep breaths to relax. Meditation will help accomplish some very positive results for you. Don't be in a hurry to leave this special time for yourself. Make sure you alott quality time for your own personal peace and growth.

COUPLE/FAMILY ~

If you are a couple or family, along with each doing the exercise above as an individual, I would encourage you to do this together with the goal of becoming a powerful team to advance in life and relationships beyond what you even thought was possible. Allow yourselves as a family to hold each other accountable for growth.

As a couple/family, commit first to NO JUDGING, ONLY ENCOURAGEMENT, and WHAT PERSONAL INFORMATION IS SHARED IN THE FAMILY, STAYS WITHIN THE FAMILY! Confidentiality is the key! You can only share with others the good things that are taking place within YOU.

GROUP ~

Do this with a group of people, i.e., friends, church groups, exercise groups, work groups, etc. following the same guidelines as a family above, and then willingly allow yourselves to be accountable to each other for your growth. As a group, commit first to NO JUDGING, ONLY ENCOURAGEMENT, and WHAT PERSONAL INFORMATION IS SHARED IN THE GROUP, STAYS WITHIN THE GROUP! Confidentiality is the key! You can only share with others the good things that are taking place within you .

Finally;

I believe for great success and rewards in every area of your life as you commit to becoming the most amazing you that you are purposed to be!

Believing In & For You,

Cliff

Inspired Mind

Transformed Thinking

Think on what is true, honorable, just, pure, lovely, commendable, excellent, and praiseworthy!

Keep your mind focused on these things and your life adventure will be epic.

Mindset is the internal force that molds and makes us.

~ Cliff Wilt

Will you do this journey with an open mind and deep commitment to become the positively best you that was originally purposed for you before birth ?

Today I Am Grateful For :

I Challenge Myself To :

No matter what we face in life,

Our attitude determines our end result.

~ Cliff Wilt

Facing difficulties for maximum positive results requires us not to say 'why' but 'what'; what do I need to learn from this to make me or it better?

Today I Am Grateful For :

I Challenge Myself To :

Leading minds talk about ideas and solutions while misleading minds talk about people and things.

~ Cliff Wilt

What are your main discussion topics and what can you change about the way you pick them to advance from a negative misleading mindset, to a positive leading mindset?

Today I Am Grateful For :

I Challenge Myself To :

When we reach the end of our excuses,
We have reached the beginning of something extraordinary!

~   Cliff Wilt

Our negativity is what hinders us from living the ultimate adventure of our life. What excuse(s) will you crush to begin living your extraordinary life ?

Today I Am Grateful For :

I Challenge Myself To :

.

Whatever thought challenges the peace in your mind, get rid of that thought quickly and peace will return.

~ Cliff Wilt

You have control over the length of time your peace is suspended. What can and will you do to challenge the challenge?

Today I Am Grateful For :

I Challenge Myself To :

If you change,
You will immediately set in motion a change
in the world around you. The kind of change is
your choice so choose wisely.

~   Cliff Wilt

What do you need to wisely chose to change and how will you do it ?

Today I Am Grateful For :

I Challenge Myself To :

A breakthrough in life does not come just from forces outside of us, it comes first from the force of belief within us that breakthrough is possible

~ Cliff Wilt

Our belief system is what governs our accomplishments. What beliefs will you change to see your breakthrough happen ?

Today I Am Grateful For :

I Challenge Myself To :

It is not by chance that your life gets better, it is by change.

~ Cliff Wilt

What can you do to change yourself and make that chance come into reality ?

Today I Am Grateful For :

I Challenge Myself To :

Only when we can graciously accept correction, will we be ready for learning through the university of accountability.

~ Cliff Wilt

Accountability without being receptive to correction is like trying to drive a car around a curve without turning the steering wheel. It takes correction to reach the intended destination. What correction and/or accountability are you fighting?

Today I Am Grateful For:

I Challenge Myself To:

It matters more the impact of what we accomplished than what we actually accomplished.

~ Cliff Wilt

Are you impacting in a way that will positively advance the world around you.

Today I Am Grateful For :

I Challenge Myself To :

**Seeing only the negative,
shines the spotlight of inadequacy on our
desire to appreciate.**

~ Cliff Wilt

Where do you need to increase in appreciation and see more positivity ?

Today I Am Grateful For :

I Challenge Myself To :

~ Notes ~

The instrument of positive possibility,
Will drown out the orchestra of defeat

~ Cliff Wilt

What positive thoughts will you adopt to drown out the orchestra of defeat ?

Today I Am Grateful For :

I Challenge Myself To :

When we rely on others to make our life matter, There will always be something the matter with our life.

~ Cliff Wilt

What are you willing to do today to value yourself and not look to others for that validation ?

Today I Am Grateful For :

I Challenge Myself To :

.

Focusing on possibilities
Turns hindrances into opportunities

~ Cliff Wilt

What possible opportunities are you not seeing in your present life hindrances ?

Today I Am Grateful For :

I Challenge Myself To :

Our focus determines the direction of our energy.

~ Cliff Wilt

Are you maintaining your focus in the positive direction you want your life to flow in ?

Today I Am Grateful For :

I Challenge Myself To :

Emotional energy is valuable, Spend it wisely

~   Cliff Wilt

Be selective about what you allow to feed off of your emotions. Once spent, there is no refund. Where do you need to get control of your emotions ?

Today I Am Grateful For :

I Challenge Myself To:

34

Commitment to self is only valuable
When it positively impacts the world around
you.

~ Cliff Wilt

Pride ill defined brings about destruction. Where do you need to
address your pride ?

Today I Am Grateful For :

I Challenge Myself To :

Do not let the fact of being right feed the attitude of superiority.

~ Cliff Wilt

Be careful to not find your significance at the expense of others. When it isn't a life or death matter, are you willing to concede, even if you think you are right ?

Today I Am Grateful For :

I Challenge Myself :

Motive is the thermometer
of the heart

~ Cliff Wilt

If your motive is pure, the heart thermometer will be at the ideal temperature. What is your real heart temperature and what can you do to keep your temp stable ?

Today I Am Grateful For :

I Challenge Myself To :

~ Notes ~

Appreciation is
the foundation of contentment

~ Cliff Wilt

Building upon appreciation will produce walls of contentment and a covering of peace. What can you do to be more appreciative ?

Today I Am Grateful For :

I Challenge Myself To :

Valuable relationships are not defined by what we receive, but by what we invest.

~ Cliff Wilt

Relationship value is not in what we receive for what we pay, but in what we are willing to pay for what we receive. How do your investments look truthfully ?

Today I Am Grateful For :

I Challenge Myself To:

Disappointment is drowned in the sea of Gratefulness

~ Cliff Wilt

Being grateful sees the gift rather than the cost. Truthfully, how accurate is your evaluator ?

Today I Am Grateful For :

I Challenge Myself To :

Treasuring the right things in life, brings increasing joy to the heart

~   Cliff Wilt

It's closet cleaning time in your heart. Holding things in our heart that do not belong there are destructive to everyone. What junk in your heart needs to go?

Today I Am Grateful For :

I Challenge Myself To :

Fruitful Giving, is the essence of a well lived life.

~ Cliff Wilt

Our lack of feeling significant can simply come from withholding from the world around us that which we have been gifted to give. What are you withholding that you need to give instead ?

Today I Am Grateful For :

I Challenge Myself To:

We have embraced the core heart of life, not when we have been loved unconditionally, but when we have unconditionally loved.

~ Cliff Wilt

You will not be complete until you have unconditionally loved someone whom you feel doesn't deserve it. Who do you need to unconditionally love now, and what do you need to do to show it ?

Today I Am Grateful For :

I Challenge Myself To :

The most powerful tool for accomplishment in our lives, is what we believe to be possible.

~ Cliff Wilt

All things are possible to those who believe. Where in your life do you need to exercise this more ?

Today I am Grateful For :

I Challenge Myself To :

Humility is owning more than your part of the blame, and accepting less than your part of the credit.

~ Cliff Wilt

What is your Ego quotient number ? In what positive ways can you reduce that number ?

Today I Am Grateful For :

I Challenge Myself To :

Contentment is achieved, when we joyfully embrace the process of life.

~ Cliff Wilt

How can you be joyful, in spite of your circumstances.

Today I Am Grateful For :

Personal Challenge Myself To :

~ *Notes* ~

Joy comes when we choose to count our blessings, and not our problems.

~   Cliff Wilt

What joys are you robbing yourself of?

Today I Am Grateful For :

I Challenge Myself To :

"Hope" ... Heavens response when there seems to be no earthly reason.

~ Cliff Wilt

Without hope, we cannot fully appreciate our life path. What do you need to renew your hope in ?

Today I Am Grateful For :

I Challenge Myself To :

Challenge exists to help us soar, our altitude is determined by our Attitude.

~   Cliff Wilt

What is your SLA (soaring level attitude) ?

Today I Am Grateful For :

I Challenge Myself To :

The challenge of life, is to live it in a way that inspires others.

~ Cliff Wilt

In what ways are you being a positive inspiration to others?

Today I Am Grateful For :

I Challenge Myself To :

One good thing done today, will powerfully and positively impact tomorrow.

~   Cliff Wilt

What is your plan for a daily good accomplishment ?

Today I Am Grateful For :

I Challenge Myself To :

Meaningful progress happens when we bloom where we're planted.

~ Cliff Wilt

What kind of progress are you after?

Today I Am Grateful For :

I Challenge Myself To :

When we focus on the difficulty, we lose;
When we focus on the positive that can be
gained, everyone wins.

~ Cliff Wilt

You are always just one more try away from victory!

Today I Am Grateful For :

I Challenge Myself To :

If you think something is impossible to do, stay out of the way and do not hinder those who are willing to make it happen.

~ Cliff Wilt

Often we underestimate our abilities and give up to easily to defeat. What do you need to recommit to starting or finishing ?

Today I Am Grateful For :

I Challenge Myself To :

A life well lived, leaves a legacy of giving, grace, and unconditional love.

~ Cliff Wilt

What kind of contributions are you making to your legacy ?

If little or nothing, what will you commit to start contributing now ?.

Today I Am Grateful For :

I Challenge Myself To :

~ Notes ~

Success comes
when excuses are crushed
with calculated action.

~ Cliff Wilt

What action can you develop a working plan about, that will not allow for anything but a successful conclusion ?

Today I Am Grateful For :

I Challenge Myself To :

When we love what we do,
We are energized by it.

~ Cliff Wilt

If you are not doing what you love to do, energize yourself with the fact that you can still make it happen while you wait. What are you waiting for ?

Today I Am Grateful For :

I Challenge Myself To :

The bright light in any negative situation, is the positive that you choose to see.

~ Cliff Wilt

What do you need to change within yourself to improve your sight ?

Today I Am Grateful For :

I Challenge Myself To :

**Intrinsic value never changes,
only perceived value can change; perceived will
never be as accurate as intrinsic.**

~ Cliff Wilt

Is the value you see in others their intrinsic value, or your perceived value ?

Today I Am Grateful For :

I Challenge Myself To :

Don't buy in to some one else's plan for your life, forge your own path to your higher calling.

~ Cliff Wilt

If you're clear about your calling, are you forging your path, or stuck in a rut ? What is your next step and how will you take it ?

Today I Am Grateful For :

I Challenge Myself To :

You are the master of your thoughts. Only you can control them.

~ Cliff Wilt

No one can make you think what you don't want to think. What will you do to exercise positive mind control ?

Today I Am Grateful For :

I Challenge Myself To :

The pain of our trials,
is the fuel of our victories.

~ Cliff Wilt

What pain or trial are you in right now that you can change your view of it to fuel your expectation of the coming victory?

Today I Am Grateful for :

I Challenge Myself To :

As beauty is in the eye of the beholder, value is in the heart of the discerner.

~ Cliff Wilt

What value do you need to discern in yourself or others that you have been neglecting ?

Today I Am Grateful For :

I Challenge Myself To :

The house of gratefulness is built on the foundation of love.

~ Ciff Wilt

What is your foundation, and what kind of house are you building on it?

Today I Am Grateful For :

I Challenge Myself To :

~ Notes ~

If we surround ourselves with only those who are like us, we will never be challenged to grow beyond where we are.

~ Cliff Wilt

Check your inner circle. Are there are enough differences to cause you to be challenged to grow beyond where you are now ?

Today I Am Grateful For :

I Challenge Myself To :

Two attitudes
that govern the quality of our
choices in daily life situations are;
Self Focused or Others Focused.

~ Cliff Wilt

Which attitude usually governs your choices ? Are you in need of an attitude adjustment for your own good and the good of others ?

Today I Am Grateful For :

I Challenge Myself To :

Your giftings and talents shed light on your purpose, and sharing them allows that light to shine brighter.

~ Cliff Wilt

What are you holding back that is meant to contribute positively to the world around you?

Today I Am Grateful For :

I Challenge Myself To :

Personal growth is a challenge not a demand, and it is not for the faint of heart.

~ Cliff Wilt

What do you need to grow in, and will you commit to the challenge ?

Today I Am Grateful For :

I Challenge Myself To :

Two of the greatest drives we can have is for learning and transforming.

~ Cliff Wilt

What are you driven to, and is it making a positive impact in you and in the world around you ?

Today I Am Grateful For :

I Challenge Myself To :

**When we refuse to change
we are refusing to grow.
What doesn't grow, dies.**

~ Cliff Wilt

What change do you need to give in to so that you can become your best self ?

Today I Am Grateful For :

I Challenge Myself To :

**Everything good done for someone else,
is a joy seed planted in the garden of your soul.**

~ Cliff Wilt

What good seeds can you plant today to enrich your soul garden ?

Today I Am Grateful For :

I Challenge Myself To :

The mind controls the body, if the head is not right, the rest of the body will be out of joint.

~ Cliff Wilt

What adjustments need to be made to your thinking and doing that will allow the body to be in sync and harmony again ?

Today I Am Grateful For :

I Challenge Myself To :

Action is the high octane fuel for Results.

~ Cliff Wilt

What grade of growth fuel are you using; low grade, mid grade, or high octane? You have control of the pump !

Today I Am Grateful For :

I Challenge Myself To :

~ Notes ~

A **ME** Focused life creates a life of
Miserable **E**xistence where contentment and
peace elude you. A **WE** focused life creates a
life of **W**inning **E**xistence where contentment and
peace are a natural byproduct.

~ Cliff Wilt

ME life or WE life ? The outcome and choice is yours. What can you deny yourself about and pick up the cause of someone else and cheer them on?

Today I Am Grateful For :

I Challenge Myself To :

When it comes to success, if time is of the essence, then change is overdue.

~ Cliff Wilt

Whatever you procrastinate on is probably the most important thing that needs to be accomplished. **Now** is the best time to start. What is it and Will You do it now ?

Today I Am Grateful For :

I Challenge Myself To :

The grit of adversity polishes the jewel of perseverence.

~ Cliff Wilt

What are you uncomfortable with or in right now that you need to accept as something that will eventually help you to shine ?

Today I Am Grateful For :

I Challenge Myself To :

It's ok to be rubbed the wrong way, the friction will bring beauty to the grain of your character.

~ Cliff Wilt

What character trait do you need to grow in from the friction heat in your life ?

Today I Am Grateful For :

I Challenge Myself To :

Do not give mileage to negative thinking, it will be a long, tiring trip, and you will quickly run out of gas.

~   Cliff Wilt

What do you need to change in your thinking today that will put you on the positive road to emotional freedom and endless energy ?

Today I Am Grateful For :

I Challenge Myself To :

Life is not about how long you live, it's about how you live that matters.

~ Cliff Wilt

What can you do to shift focus from concern about length of your life, to accomplished legacy of your life?

Today I Am Grateful For :

I Challenge Myself To :

If you think you cannot change the world because you're only one, think again. A single vision caught by a few has always been the catalyst to a world change.

~ Cliff Wilt

What are you doing to fulfill your specific purpose in this life ?
If nothing, what can you do, or what more can you do ?

Today I Am Grateful For :

I Challenge Myself To :

Your mind's eye believes,
what your perception eye interprets.

~ Cliff Wilt

What needs to change about how you perceive things, to make sure that what you believe is actually true ?

Today I Am Grateful For :

I Challenge Myself To :

Life experiences will make you bitter or better depending upon your belief system around the lesson to be learned.

~ Cliff Wilt

What life story are you subscribing to ? What must you change about your story to refocus yourself on a brighter future ?

Today I Am Grateful For :

I Challenge Myself To :

~ Notes ~

**What matters more than the way you think,
is what you think, because what you think
determines the way you think.**

~ Cliff Wilt

What you think determines the way you think. You have the power
to change your thoughts to create a lifetime of positive impact. What
thoughts can you change now to positively affect the different areas
of your life.

Today I Am Grateful For :

I Challenge Myself To :

Over indulging comes from over thinking.

~ Cliff Wilt

You get more of whatever you are focused on. What focus must you change to effect a decrease in over indulging in things harmful to you?

Today I Am Graetful For :

I Challenge Myself To :

If your thoughts are not serving you positively, Think Again!

~ Cliff Wilt

What thought do you have that is not encouragingly inspiring you ?
Replace it now with a thought that will !

Today I Am Grateful For :

I Challenge Myself To :

You live your life on full,
When You live your life full on

~ Cliff Wilt

Only you can determine for yourself what your fulfilled life looks like. Envision the path for your fulfilled life then go full speed on that path to accomplishment. What is that path for you ?

Today I Am Grateful For :

I Challenge Myself To :

How a person thinks in their heart, is how they are.

~ Cliff Wilt

Your heart has the ability to think. What do you need to change in your heart to bring about a better attitude for your life and those around you ?

Today I Am Grateful For :

I Challenge Myself To :

The more you encourage the value in the lives of those around you, the more valuable you become.

~   Cliff Wilt

Where and to whom can you add value remembering to deflect glory.

Today I Am Grateful For :

I Challenge Myself To :

Every negative thought steals positive energy that was intended for accomplishing your ultimate life purpose.

~ Cliff Wilt

What negative thoughts do you need to get control over ?

Today I Am Grateful For :

I Challenge Myself To :

Peace is a state of mind that you control by what you focus on.

~ Cliff Wilt

What focus do you need to change to bring about a peaceful state ?

Today I Am Grateful For :

I Challenge Myself To :

Peace of mind happens when we do not allow negative circumstances without, to dictate to our governing heart within.

~ Cliff Wilt

What circumstances are You allowing to negatively influence your thought process, and what will you do within yourself to stop it and change it to positive influence ?

Today I Am Grateful For :

I Challenge Myself To :

~ *Notes* ~

You cannot go backwards and start over, but you can start a change in forward momentum now to achieve a new outcome.

~ Cliff Wilt

Are you wasting energy on the past? What will you do to rewrite your today for a brighter tomorrow ?

Today I Am grateful For :

I Challenge Myself To :

When we exercise and strengthen the muscle of gratitude, We weaken the arthritis of complaint.

~ Cliff Wilt

Complaining, like arthritis, is cripiling. Being fully grateful for the blessing, which is 'life', increases our sensitivity to others needs around us. What are those needs, and what can you do now to be a catlayst of positive change for those needs?

Today I Am Grateful For :

I Challenge Myself To :

The most rewarding life investment made,
is making consistent deposits of
encouragement in the life of others.

~ Cliff Wilt

Now is a good time to start making consistent positive deposits in the life of others? With whom and in what way could you start now?

Today I Am Grateful For :

I Challenge Myself To :

The most profitable commitment you can make
in your life for your ultimate success, is the
commitment to change.

~ Cliff Wilt

What do you need to commit to change, not in your circumstances,
but in yourself to achieve your ultimate life success ?

Today I Am Grateful For :

I Challenge Myself To :

Good intentions are not proven by desire or willingness, but by purposed action.

~ Cliff Wilt

What is it that you have been intending to do, that you could now purpose to do for the benefit of others and the stress release for yourself?

Today I Am Gratefule For :

I Challenge Myself To :

The sum of all that you are is derived from the type and amount of growth you allow in every area of your life.

~ Cliff Wilt

What type and amount of growth in your life will you allow, to become the best you for the benefit of the world around you and yourself ?

Today I Am Grateful For :

I Challenge Myself To :

The most powerful control we can have, is to be in complete control of oneself.

~ Cliff Wilt

Where do you need to get more control over yourself personally ?

Today I Am Gratefule For :

I Challenge Myself To :

There is no one so blind as the one whom has sight but refuses to see.

~ Cliff Wilt

In what area of your life does there need to be change that you are refusing to accept that the change starts with you ?

Today I Am Grateful For :

I Challenge Myself To :

The honest self-examining chisel of truth,
if allowed, will shape us for
what we are purposed for.

~   Cliff Wilt

Be honest now ... Are you being completely honest with yourself ?
Ask an immediate family member or someone you know who will be
honest with you.

Today I Am Grateful For :

I Challenge Myself To :

~ Notes ~

The only journey that cannot be completed, is the one that is not started.

~ Cliff Wilt

What steps can you commit to take now to stop holding yourself back from reaching your destiny.

Today I Am Gratefule For :

I Challenge Myself To :

Little sacrifices create little successes, great sacrifices create great successes.

~ Cliff Wilt

How successful do you want to be and what is your willing sacrifice personally ?

Today I Am Grateful For :

I Challenge Myself To :

As desire and action is the fuel for procurement, aspiration and action is the fuel for achievement.

~ Cliff Wilt

What are you desiring for and aspiring to ? How will your personal life and the world be better for it ?

Today I Am Grateful For :

I Challenge Myself To :

A mistake does not define you if you can be taught in it, strengthend by it, walked through it, and taken past it.

What do you personally need to let go of TODAY, and allow yourself to press forward to a better tomorrow ?

Today I Am Grateful For :

I Challenge Myself To :

The greatest joy in positive personal change, is understanding that it will have a positive impact on the entire world in some way.

~ Cliff Wilt

What kind of impact are you wanting and willing to make ?

Today I Am Grateful For :

I Challenge Myself To :

You will be successful when you stop kicking against circumstances intended to bring about that success.

~ Cliff Wilt

What circumstances do you need to stop fighting, and embrace for your success ?

Today I Am Grateful For :

I Challenge Myself To :

We are on the true path to wisdom when we desire to be the student more than we desire to be the teacher.

~ Cliff Wilt

Are you on the true path to wisdom?

Today I Am Grateful For :

I Challenge Myself To :

Our strength is in self-control, it gives us power to remain calm in any situation.

~ Cliff Wilt

What do you need to exercise more self-control in ?

Today I Am Grateful For :

I Challenge Myself To :

**Personal power potential is accomplished through learning,
Personal power dynamics is accomplished through application of that learning**

~   Cliff Wilt

The reason why we apply what we learn is to achieve the dynamic of who we in a positive way are purposed to become, and we can then show the way to others.

Today I Am Grateful For :

I Challenge Myself To :

Note of Thanks and Encouragement...

THANK YOU for commiting to this mind and life changing adventure. I believe if you did this whole journey with the determined goal of positive personal development and growth, you are now habitually thinking in a transforming and inspired mindset. **CONGRATULATIONS!**

I would encourage you now to recommit to going on the adventure again, and again. By keeping the notes together on the same page you can watch your own transformational and inspired growth beyond what you thought possible.

I would also encourage you to challenge your families, friends, co-workers, and others to take this journey also. They will not regret it, and they will thank you for it.

Please forward comments and/or suggestions to me at cliff@cliffwilt.com.

If you have gained benefit from this book, please leave a review for the book on Amazon.com.

Thank You again for going on this adventure with me! I look forward to hearing from you.

To Your Continued Success,

Cliff

Reminder ...

I want you to succeed, and because of that, we have put together some free resources to help you accomplish the personal success you desire. To get instant access to the free downloads, articles, and info, please visit:

www.cliffwilt.com

32337190R00069

Made in the USA
San Bernardino, CA
03 April 2016